SEQUENTIAL
JAZZ PIANO SONGS

ISBN 978-1-5400-4155-5

Visit Hal Leonard Online at
www.halleonard.com

Contact us:
Hal Leonard
7777 West Bluemound Road
Milwaukee, WI 53213
Email: info@halleonard.com

In Europe, contact:
Hal Leonard Europe Limited
42 Wigmore Street
Marylebone, London, W1U 2RN
Email: info@halleonardeurope.com

In Australia, contact:
Hal Leonard Australia Pty. Ltd.
4 Lentara Court
Cheltenham, Victoria, 3192 Australia
Email: info@halleonard.com.au

The 26 songs in this book are presented in a basic order of difficulty, beginning with the easiest arrangements (hands alone, very simple rhythms) and progressing to more difficult arrangements including hands together, syncopated rhythms and moving around the keyboard.

THE WAY YOU LOOK TONIGHT

from SWING TIME

Words by DOROTHY FIELDS
Music by JEROME KERN

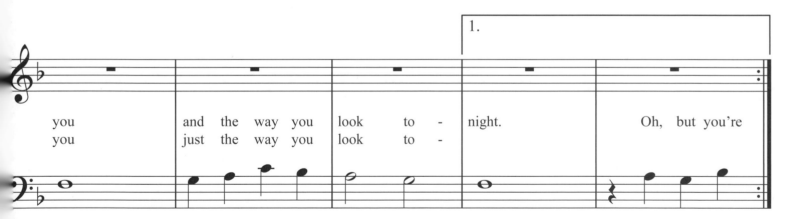

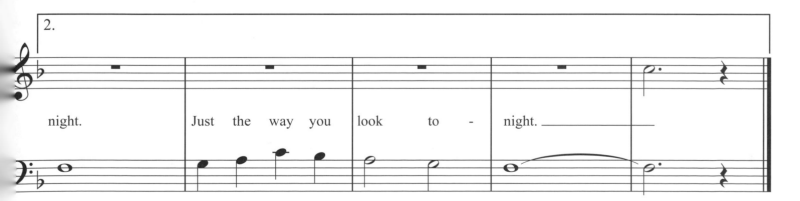

BYE BYE BLACKBIRD

from PETE KELLY'S BLUES

Words by MORT DIXON
Music by RAY HENDERSON

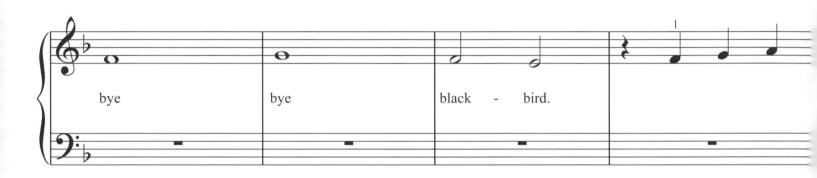

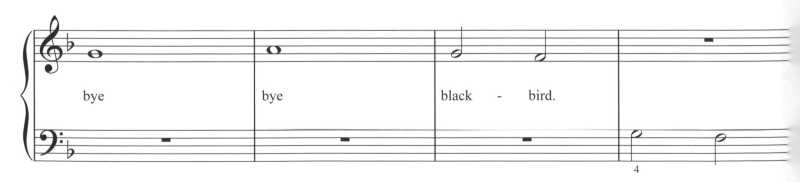

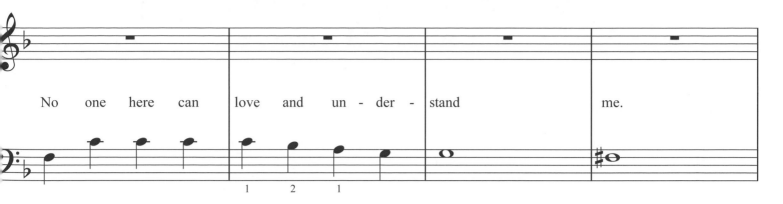

No one here can love and un - der - stand me.

Oh, what hard luck sto - ries they all hand me.

Make my bed and light the light, I'll ar - rive late to - night;

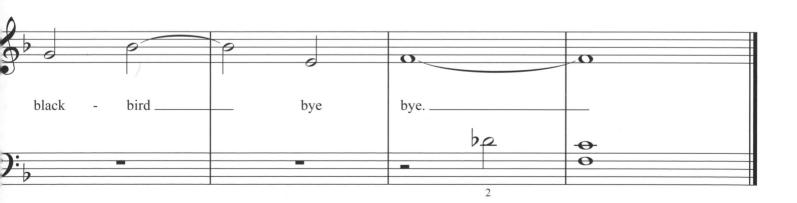

black - bird bye bye.

DAYS OF WINE AND ROSES

from DAYS OF WINE AND ROSES

Lyrics by JOHNNY MERCER
Music by HENRY MANCINI

Moderately

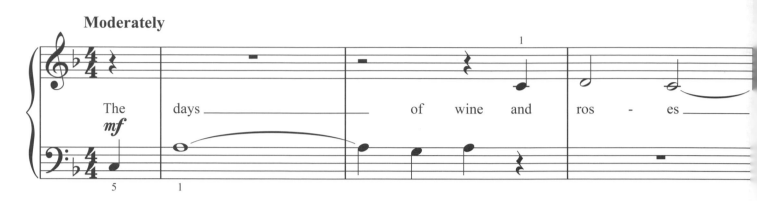

The days _____ of wine and ros - es _____

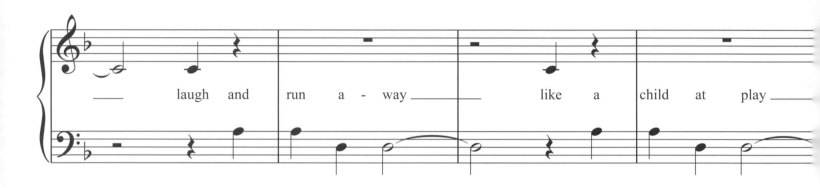

_____ laugh and run a - way _____ like a child at play

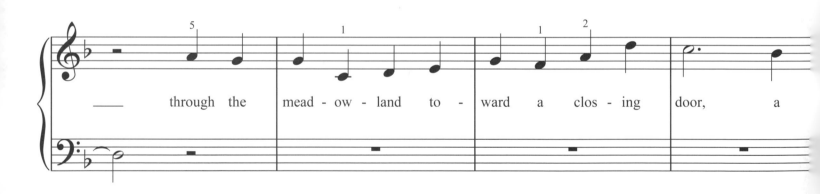

_____ through the mead - ow - land to - ward a clos - ing door, a

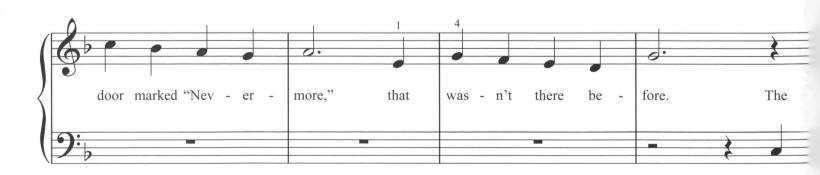

door marked "Nev - er - more," that was - n't there be - fore. The

lone - ly night dis - clos - es _____ just a

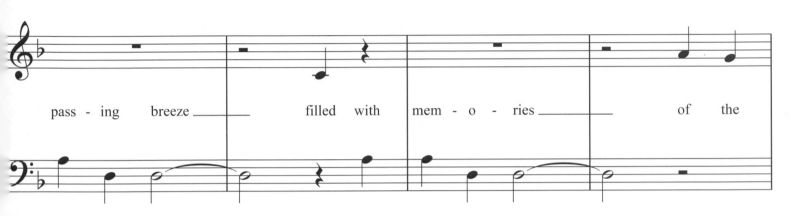

pass - ing breeze _____ filled with mem - o - ries _____ of the

gold - en smile that in - tro - duced me to _____ the

days of wine and ros - es and you.

MY FUNNY VALENTINE
from BABES IN ARMS

Words by LORENZ HART
Music by RICHARD RODGERS

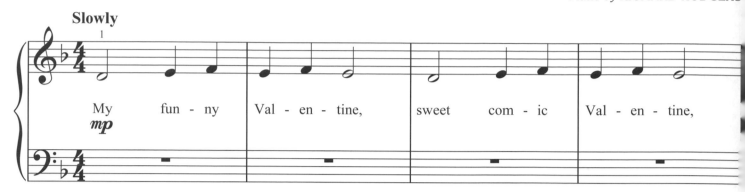

My fun - ny Val - en - tine, sweet com - ic Val - en - tine,

you make me smile with my heart. Your looks are

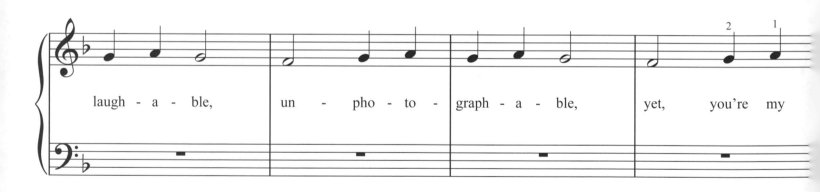

laugh - a - ble, un - pho - to - graph - a - ble, yet, you're my

fav - 'rite work of art. Is your fig - ure less than

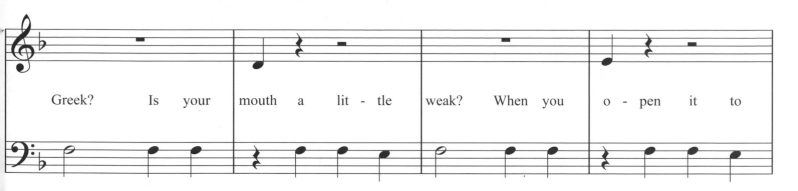

Greek? Is your mouth a lit - tle weak? When you o - pen it to

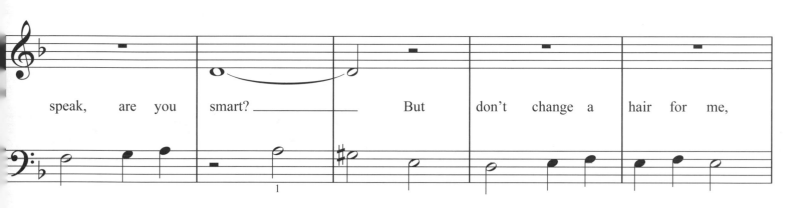

speak, are you smart? _____ But don't change a hair for me,

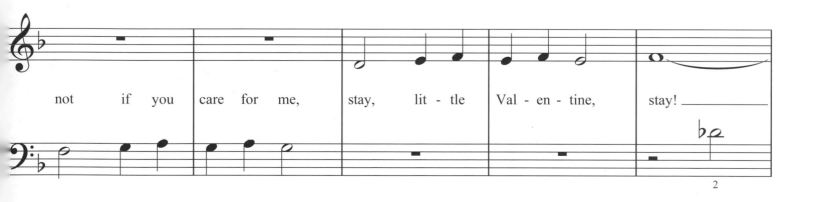

not if you care for me, stay, lit - tle Val - en - tine, stay! _____

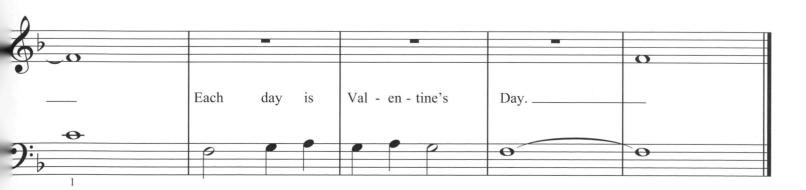

_____ Each day is Val - en - tine's Day. _____

WHEN I FALL IN LOVE

from ONE MINUTE TO ZERO

Words by EDWARD HEYMAN
Music by VICTOR YOUNG

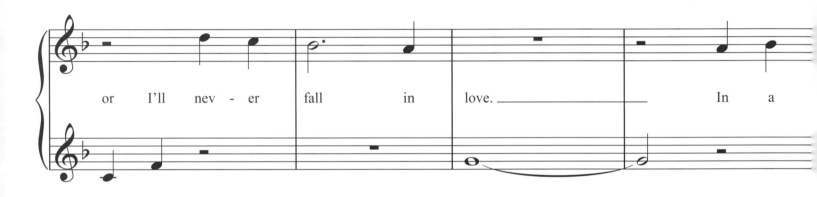

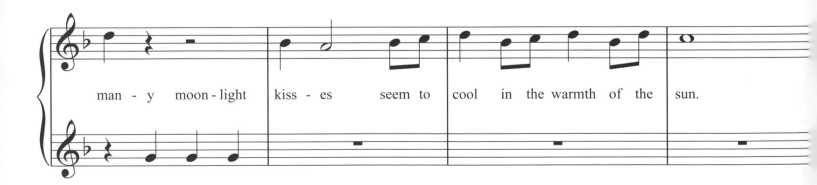

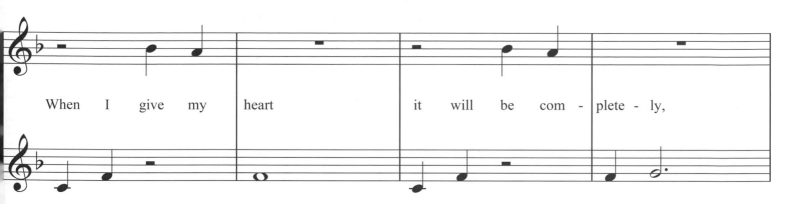

When I give my heart it will be com - plete - ly,

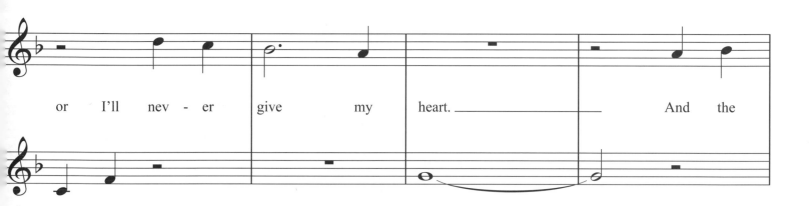

or I'll nev - er give my heart._____ And the

mo - ment I can feel that you feel that way too is

when I fall in love with you._____

FLY ME TO THE MOON
(In Other Words)
featured in the Motion Picture ONCE AROUND

Words and Music by
BART HOWARD

Moderately slow

Fly me to the moon and let me play a-mong the stars;

let me see what spring is like on Ju-pi-ter and Mars. In

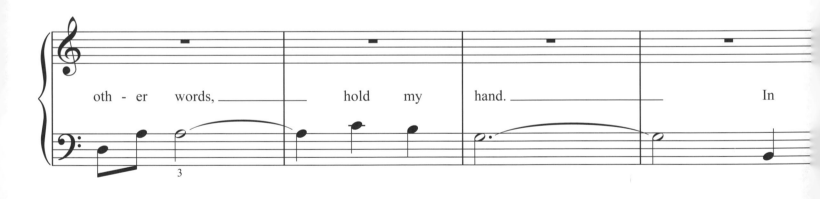

oth-er words, _____ hold my hand. _____ In

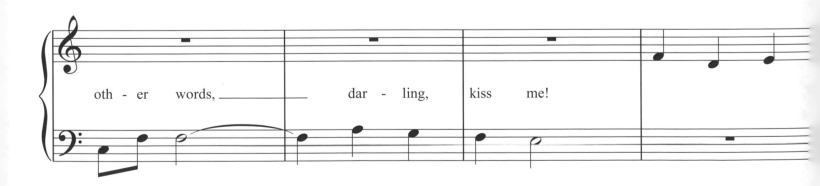

oth-er words, _____ dar-ling, kiss me!

Fill my life with song and let me sing for- ev - er more;

you are all I long for, all I wor - ship and a - dore. In

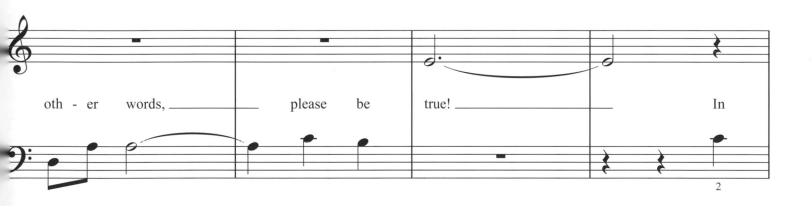

oth - er words, _____ please be true! _____ In

2

oth - er words, _____ I love you!

AUTUMN LEAVES

English lyric by JOHNNY MERCER
French lyric by JACQUES PREVERT

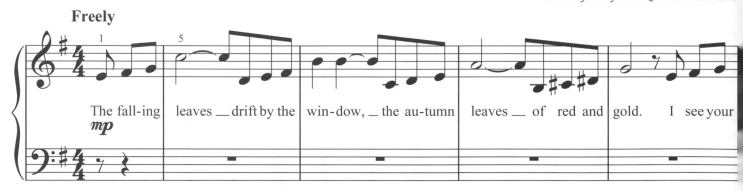

The fall-ing leaves — drift by the win-dow, — the au-tumn leaves — of red and gold. I see your

lips, —— the sum-mer kiss - es, —— the sun-burned hands —— I used to hold. Since you

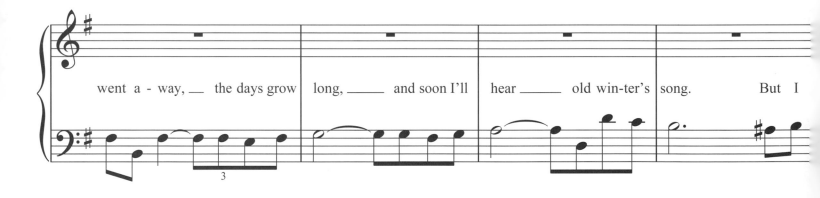

went a - way, — the days grow long, —— and soon I'll hear —— old win-ter's song. But I

miss you most of all, my dar - ling, when au - tumn leaves start to fall.

Music by Joseph Kosma
© 1947, 1950 (Renewed) ENOCH ET CIE
Sole Selling Agent for U.S. and Canada: MORLEY MUSIC CO., by agreement with ENOCH ET CIE
All Rights Reserved

BUT NOT FOR ME

from GIRL CRAZY

Music and Lyrics by GEORGE GERSHWIN
and IRA GERSHWIN

Moderately slow

- so, luck - y day!
- ler needs a friend.
Al - though I
When ev - 'ry

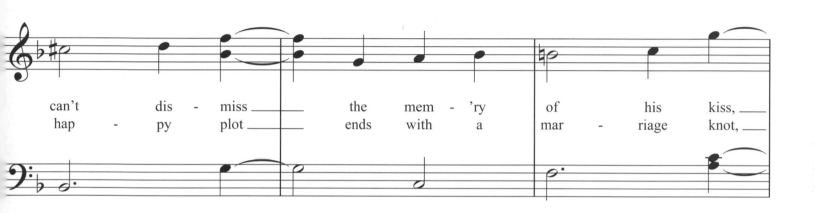

can't dis - miss the mem - 'ry of his kiss,
hap - py plot ends with a mar - riage knot,

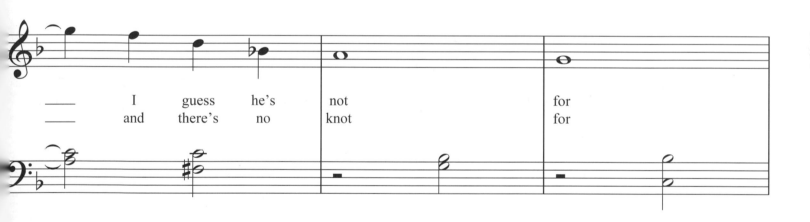

I guess he's not for
and there's no knot for

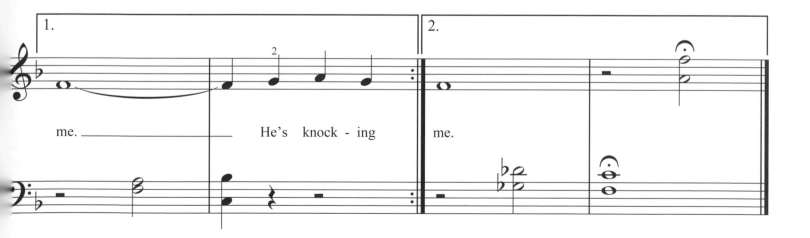

1.
me. He's knock - ing
2.
me.

THERE WILL NEVER BE
ANOTHER YOU

from the Motion Picture ICELAND

Lyric by MACK GORDON
Music by HARRY WARREN

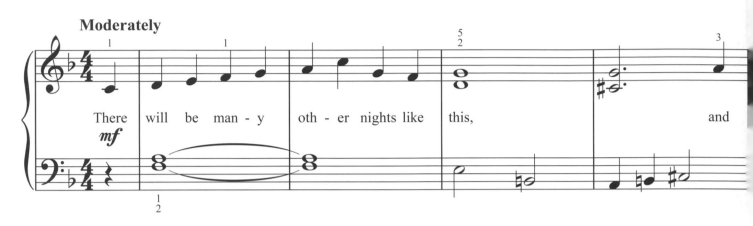

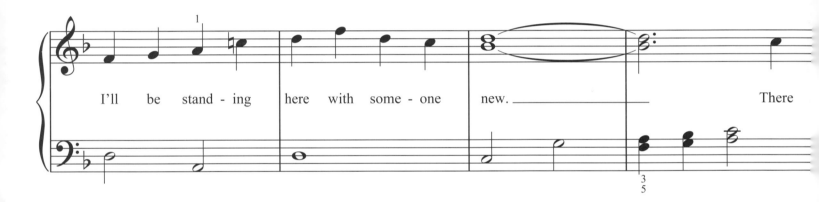

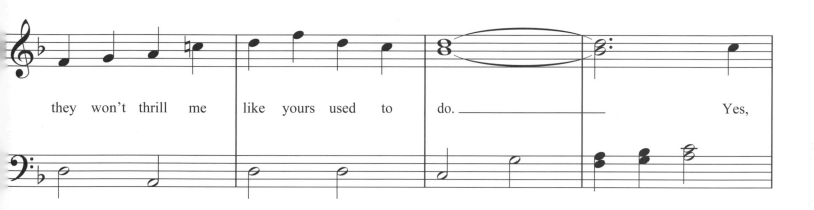

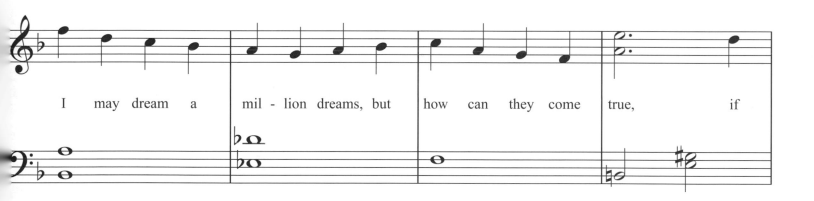

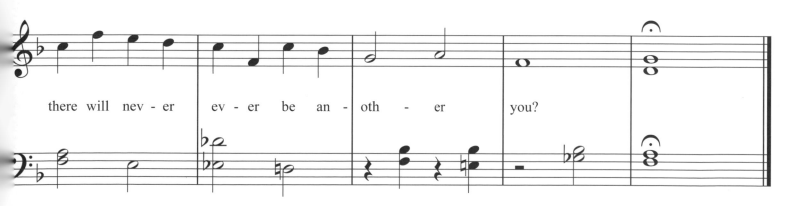

NIGHT AND DAY

from GAY DIVORCE

Words and Music by
COLE PORTER

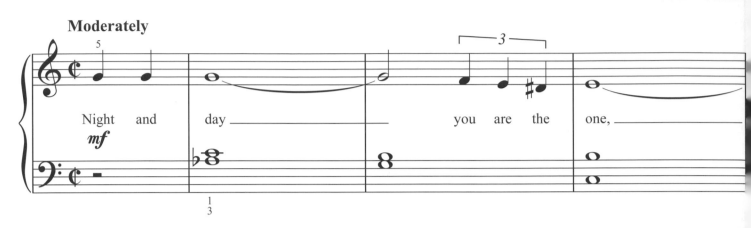

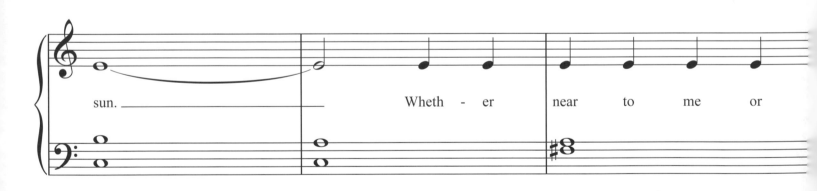

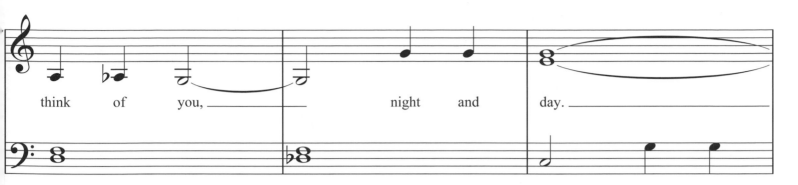

think   of   you, _____   night   and   day. _____

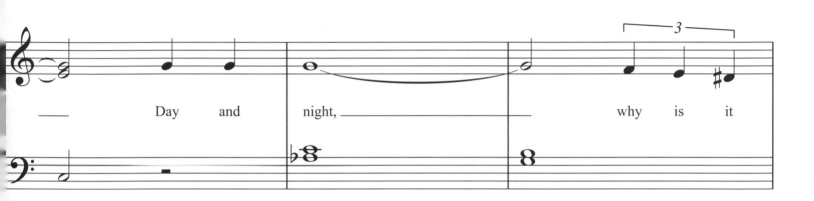

_____   Day   and   night, _____   why   is   it

so _____   that   this   long - ing   for   you

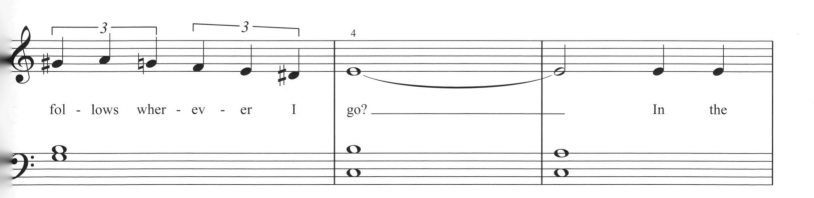

fol - lows   wher - ev - er   I   go? _____   In   the

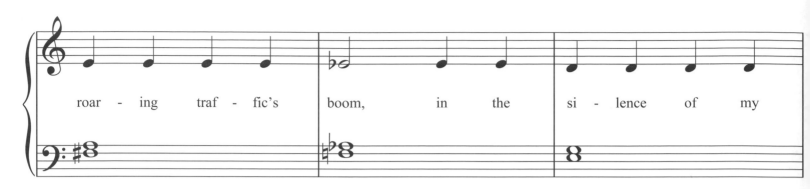

roar - ing traf - fic's boom, in the si - lence of my

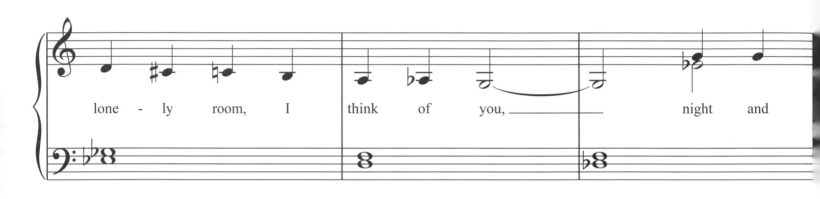

lone - ly room, I think of you, _____ night and

day. _____ Night and day, _____

_____ un - der the hide of me _____ there's an,

oh, such a hun - gry yearn - ing burn - ing in - side of me. ____

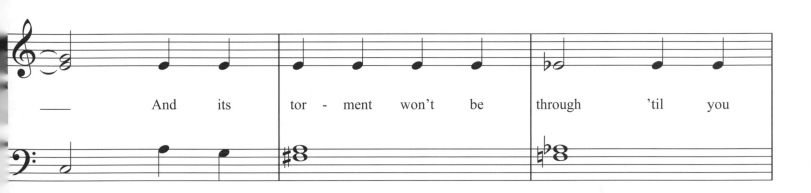

____ And its tor - ment won't be through 'til you

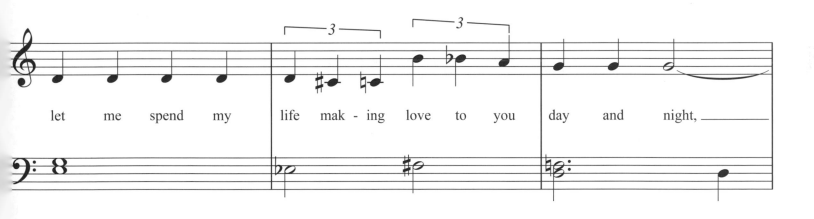

let me spend my life mak - ing love to you day and night, ____

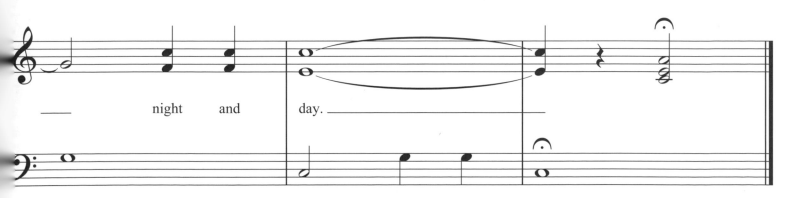

____ night and day. ____

IT COULD HAPPEN TO YOU

from the Paramount Picture AND THE ANGELS SING

Words by JOHNNY BURKE
Music by JAMES VAN HEUSEN

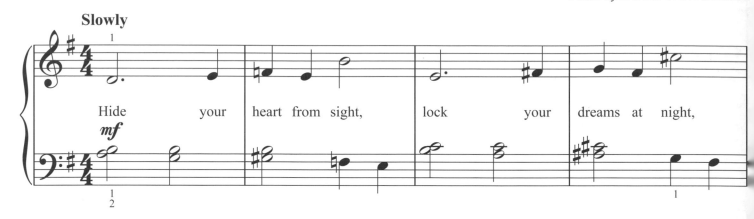

Slowly

mf

Hide your heart from sight, lock your dreams at night,

it could hap - pen to you.

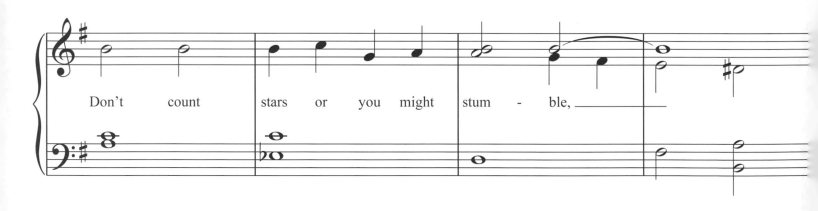

Don't count stars or you might stum - ble,

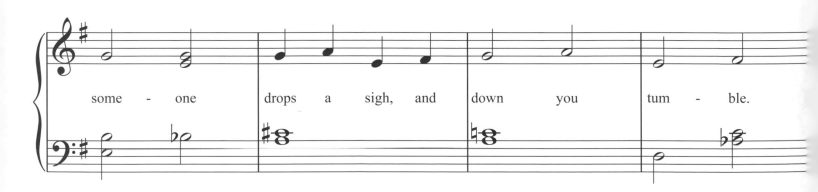

some - one drops a sigh, and down you tum - ble.

Keep an eye on spring, run when church bells ring,

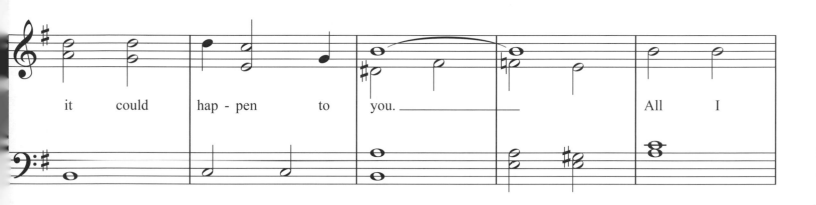

it could hap - pen to you. _____ All I

did was won - der how your arms would be, and it

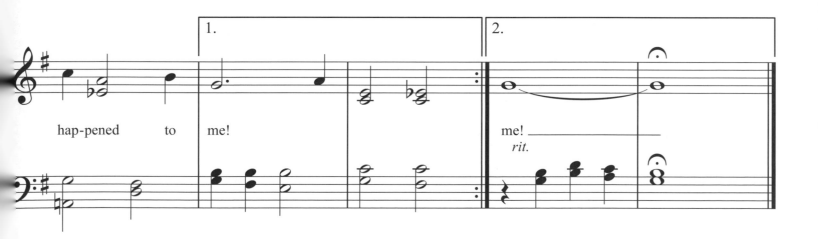

1.
hap-pened to me!

2.
me! _____
rit.

IN A SENTIMENTAL MOOD

Words and Music by DUKE ELLINGTON,
IRVING MILLS and MANNY KURTZ

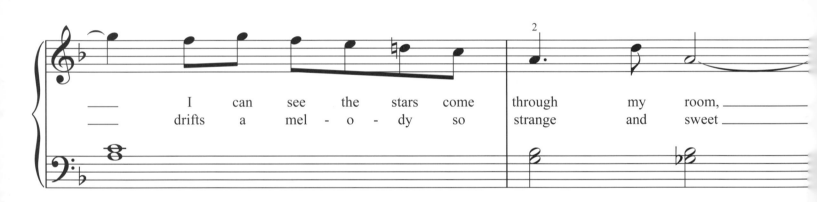

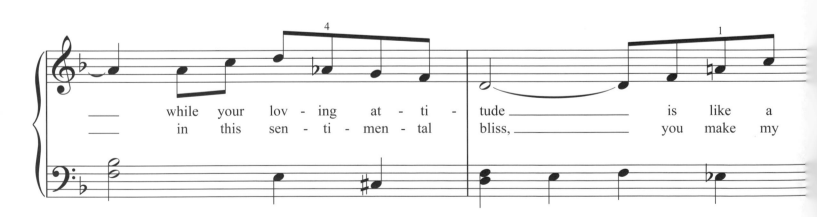

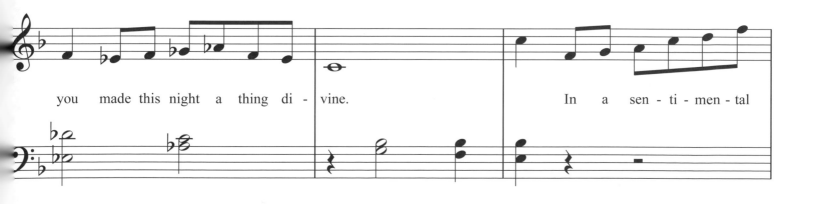

mood, _____ I'm with - in a world so heav - en - ly, _____

___ for I nev - er dreamt that you'd _____ be lov - ing

To Coda $\oplus$

D.S. al Coda
(with repeat)

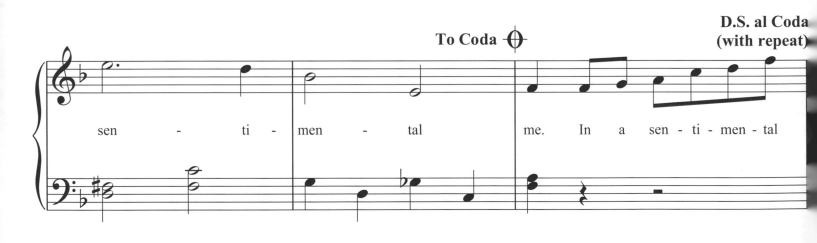

sen - ti - men - tal me. In a sen - ti - men - tal

CODA $\oplus$

me. *rit.*

ALL THE THINGS YOU ARE

from VERY WARM FOR MAY

Lyrics by OSCAR HAMMERSTEIN II
Music by JEROME KERN

Slowly, expressively

30

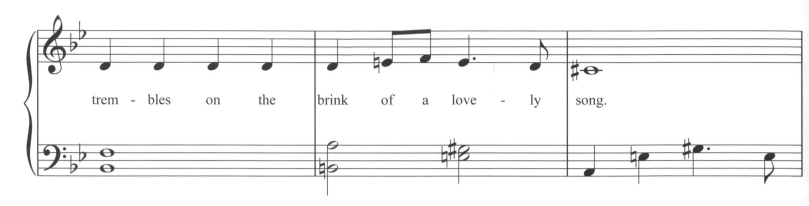

trem - bles on the brink of a love - ly song.

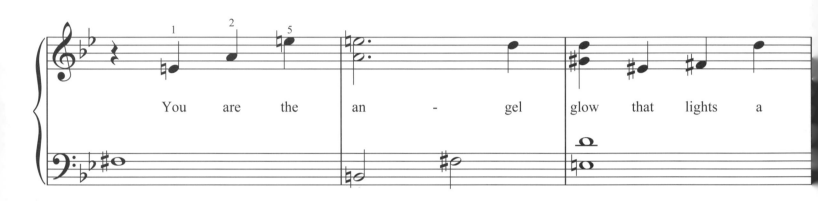

You are the an - gel glow that lights a

star. _____ The dear - est things I

know are what you are.

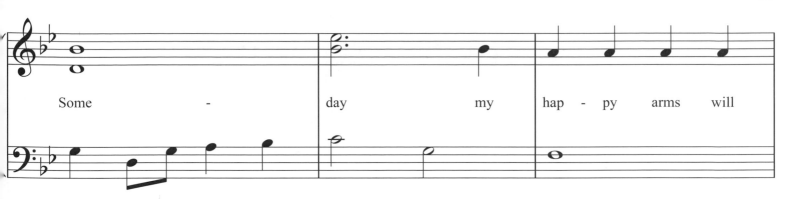

Some - day my hap - py arms will

hold you, and some - day I'll

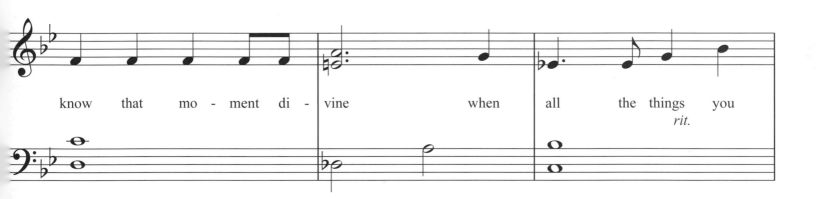

know that mo - ment di - vine when all the things you

rit.

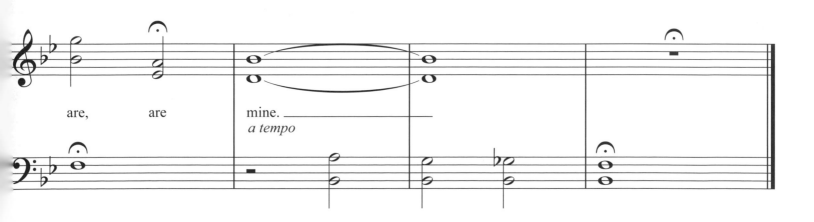

are, are mine. _____

a tempo

SOFTLY AS IN A MORNING SUNRISE
from THE NEW MOON

Lyrics by OSCAR HAMMERSTEIN II
Music by SIGMUND ROMBERG

Moderate Tango

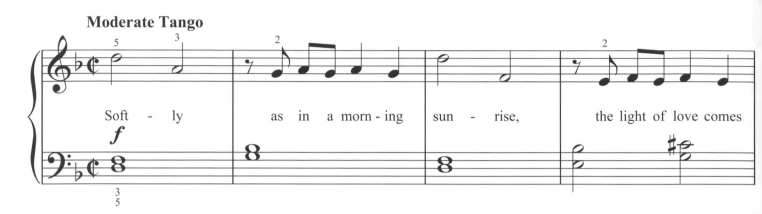

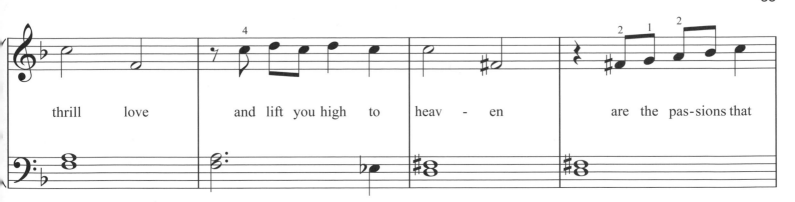

thrill love and lift you high to heav - en are the pas-sions that

kill love and let you fall to hell! So ends each sto - ry.

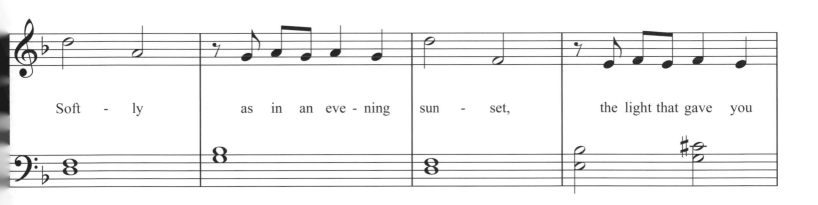

Soft - ly as in an eve - ning sun - set, the light that gave you

glo - ry will take it all a - way.

BLUESETTE

Words by NORMAN GIMBEL
Music by JEAN THIELEMANS

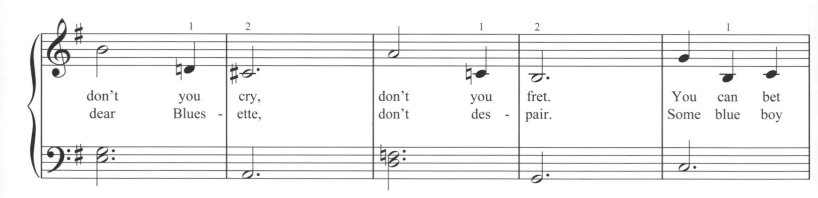

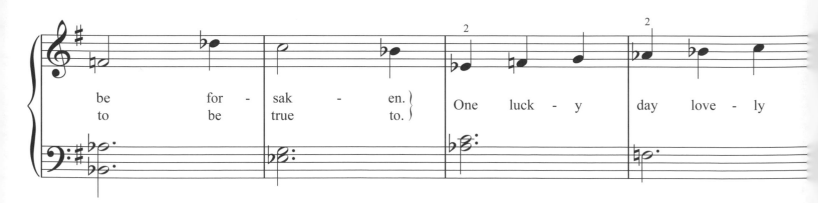

love will come your way.

way. _____ That mag - ic

day _____ may just be to - day.

MISTY

Words by JOHNNY BURKE
Music by ERROLL GARNER

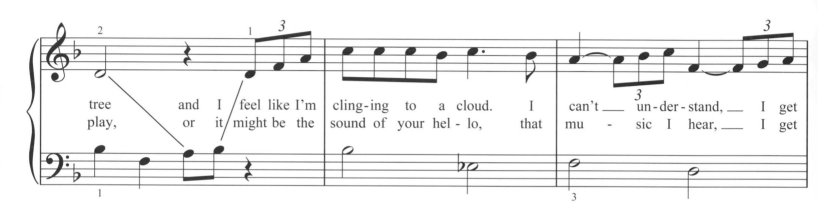

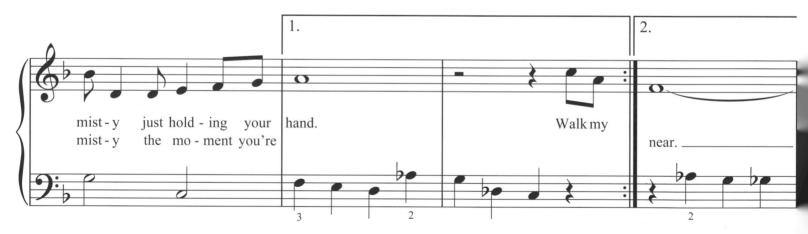

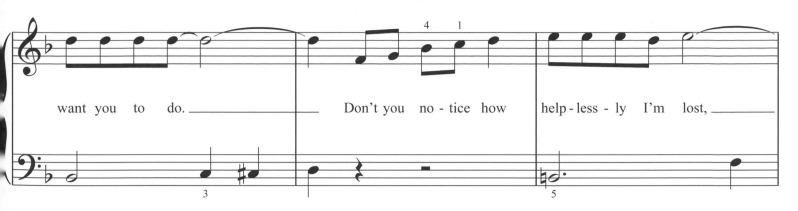

want you to do. _____ Don't you no - tice how help - less - ly I'm lost, _____

_____ that's why I'm fol - low-ing you. _____ On my own, would I

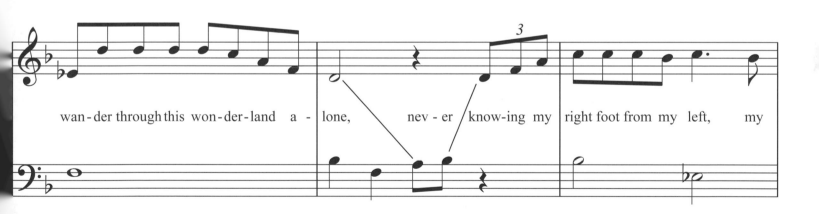

wan - der through this won - der-land a - lone, nev - er know-ing my right foot from my left, my

hat ____ from my glove? _ I'm too mist - y and too much in love. _____
rit.

THE GIRL FROM IPANEMA
(Garôta De Ipanema)

Music by ANTONIO CARLOS JOBIM
English Words by NORMAN GIMBEL
Original Words by VINICIUS DE MORAES

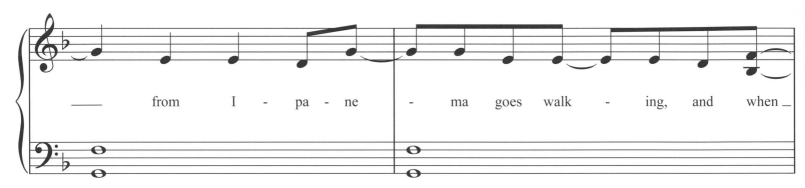

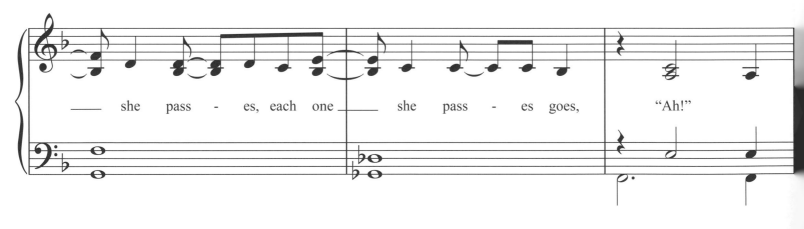

swings so cool and sways so gen - tle, that when

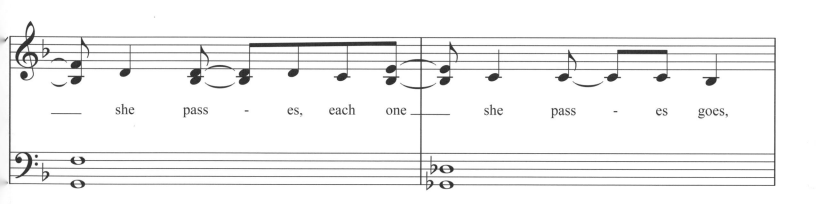

she pass - es, each one she pass - es goes,

"Ah!" Oh,

but I watch her so sad - ly.

How _____ can I tell her I love her? _____

_____ Yes, _____ I would give my heart

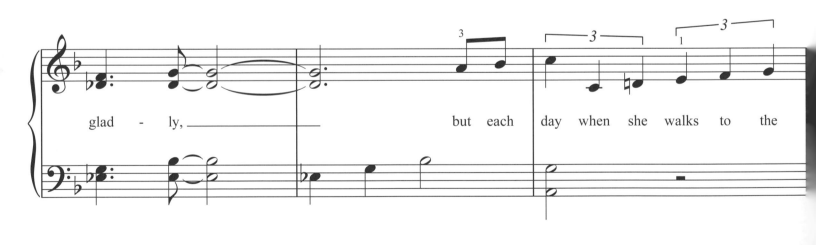

glad - ly, _____ but each day when she walks to the

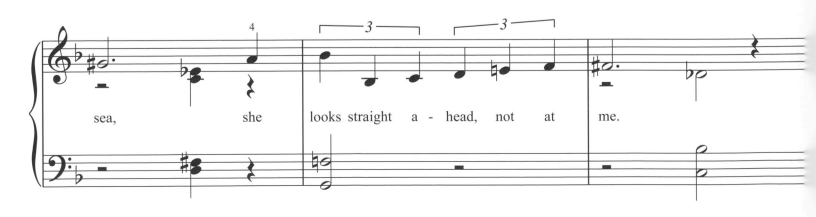

sea, she looks straight a - head, not at me.

Tall and tan and young ___ and love - ly, the girl ___ from I - pa - ne -

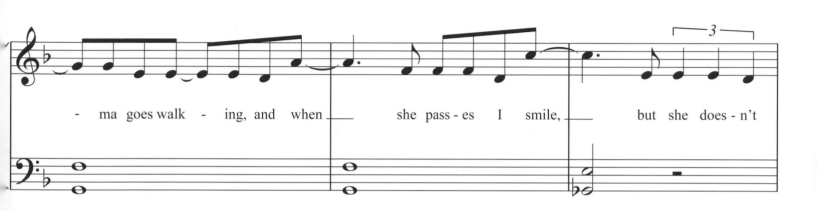

- ma goes walk - ing, and when ___ she pass - es I smile, ___ but she does - n't

see.   She just does - n't see.

No, she does - n't see.   *rit.*

SATIN DOLL

featured in SOPHISTICATED LADIES

Words by JOHNNY MERCER,
BILLY STRAYHORN and DUKE ELLINGTON
Music by DUKE ELLINGTON

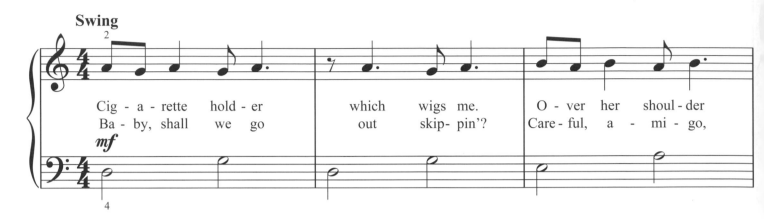

Cig - a - rette hold - er / which wigs me. / O - ver her shoul - der
Ba - by, shall we go / out skip- pin'? / Care - ful, a - mi - go,

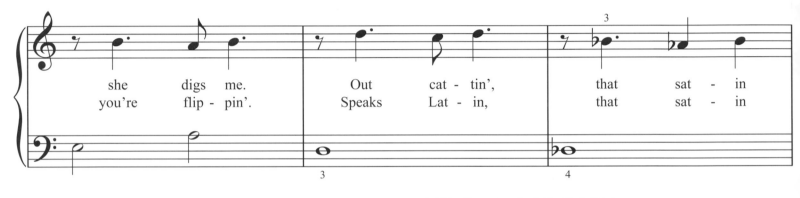

she digs me. / Out cat - tin', / that sat - in
you're flip - pin'. / Speaks Lat - in, / that sat - in

doll. / doll. / She's

no - bod - y's fool, so I'm / play - ing it cool as can / be.

I'll give it a whirl, but I ain't for no girl catch - ing

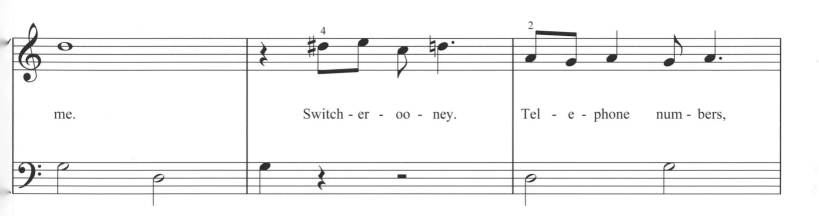

me. Switch - er - oo - ney. Tel - e - phone num - bers,

well, you know. Do - ing my rhum - bas, with u - no,

and that 'n' my sat - in doll.

AUTUMN IN NEW YORK

Words and Music by
VERNON DUKE

Moderately

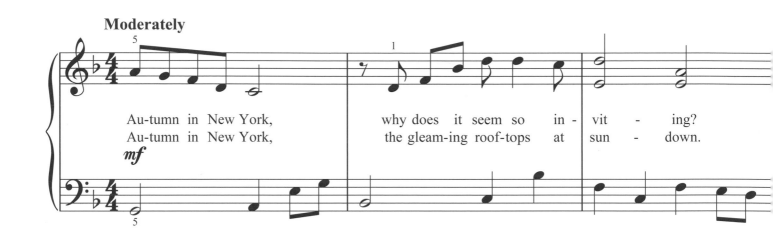

Au-tumn in New York,   why does it seem so in- vit - ing?
Au-tumn in New York,   the gleam-ing roof-tops   at sun - down.

Au-tumn in New York,   it spells the thrill of   first
Au-tumn in New York,   it lifts you up when you're

night - ing.   Glit - ter - ing crowds   and
run - down.   Jad - ed   rou - és   and

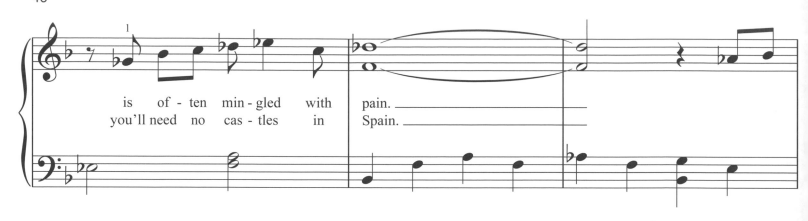

is of - ten min - gled with pain. _____
you'll need no cas - tles in Spain. _____

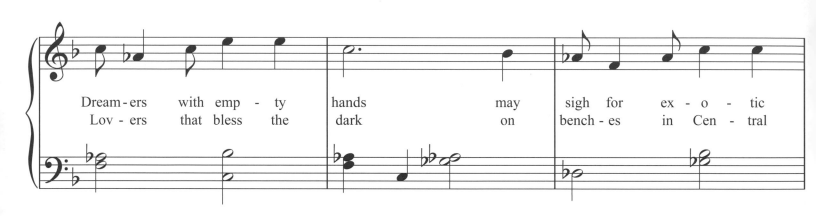

Dream - ers with emp - ty hands may sigh for ex - o - tic
Lov - ers that bless the dark on bench - es in Cen - tral

lands; it's au - tumn in New York, it's good to live it a -
Park greet au - tumn in New York; it's good to live it a -

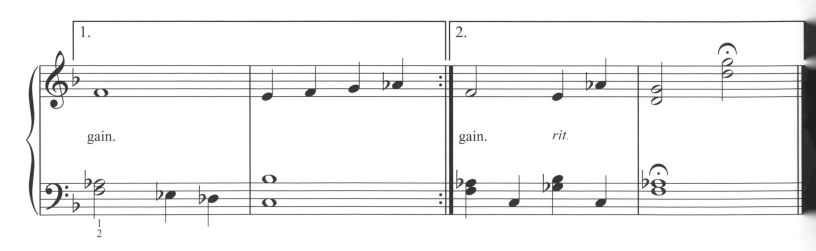

gain.

gain.   *rit.*

LULLABY OF BIRDLAND

Words by GEORGE DAVID WEISS
Music by GEORGE SHEARING

Moderate Swing

Lul - la - by of Bird-land, that's what I _____ al - ways hear _____ when you sigh. _____ Nev - er in my word-land could there be ways_ to re-veal, _____ in a phrase, _____ how I feel! _____

Have you ev - er heard two tur - tle doves _ bill and coo _

when they love? _ That's the kind of mag - ic mu - sic we make _ with our lips _

_____ when we kiss! And there's a weep-ing old wil -

- low, _____ he real - ly knows how to cry. _

I GOT RHYTHM

from AN AMERICAN IN PARIS

Music and Lyrics by GEORGE GERSHWIN
and IRA GERSHWIN

Moderately, somewhat rubato

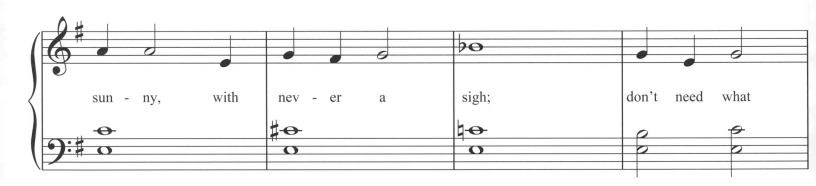

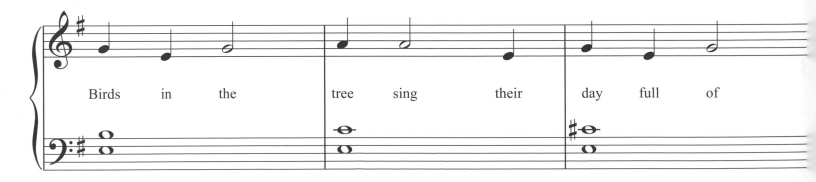

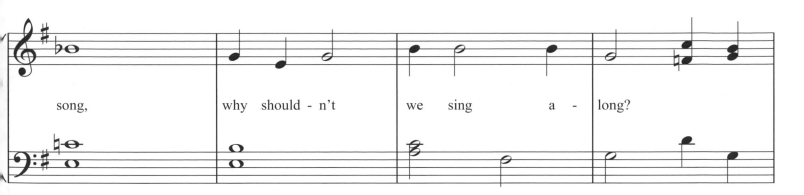

song,   why should - n't   we   sing   a -   long?

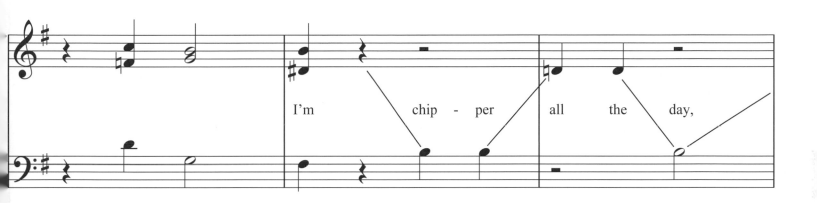

I'm   chip - per   all   the   day,

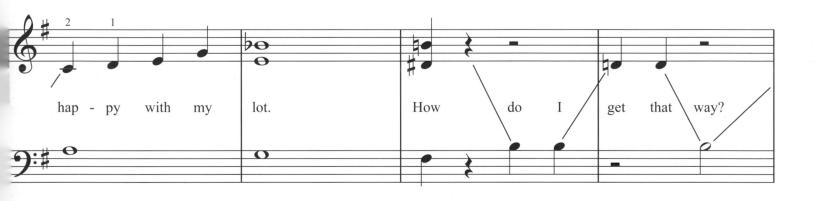

hap - py with my   lot.   How   do   I   get that way?

Look   at what I've   got:

Lively

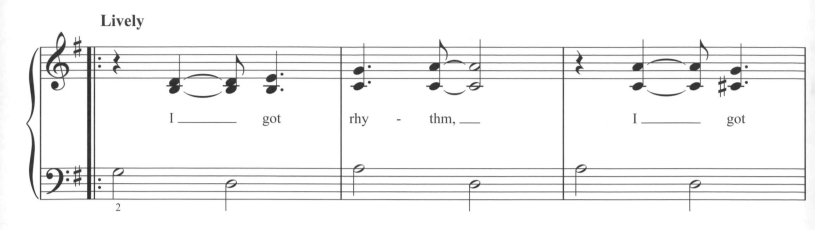

I _____ got rhy - thm, ___ I _____ got

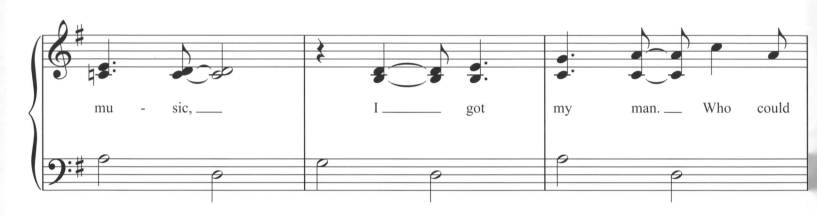

mu - sic, ___ I _____ got my man. ___ Who could

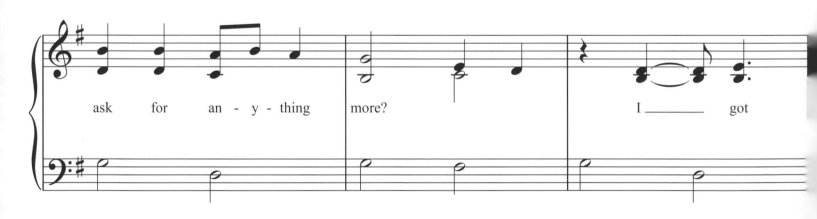

ask for an - y - thing more? I _____ got

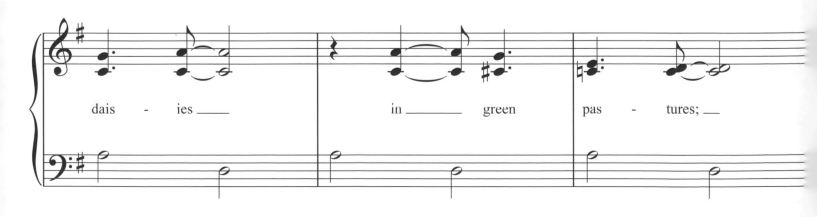

dais - ies _____ in _____ green pas - tures; ___

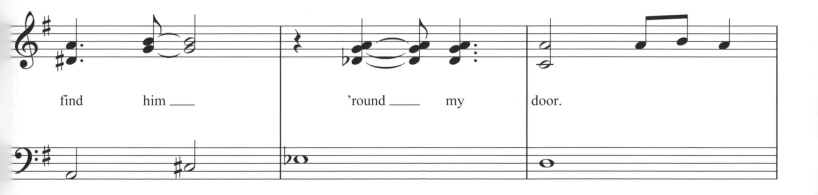

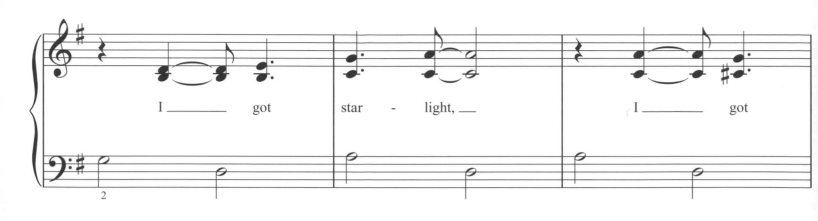

I _____ got star - light, _____ I _____ got

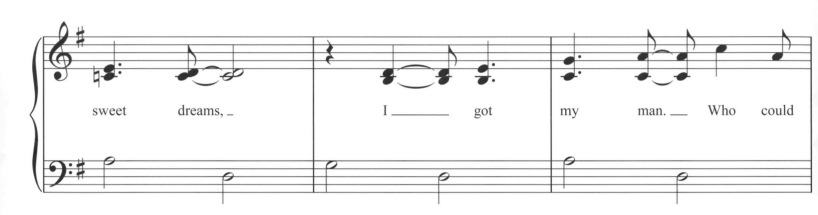

sweet dreams, _ I _____ got my man. _ Who could

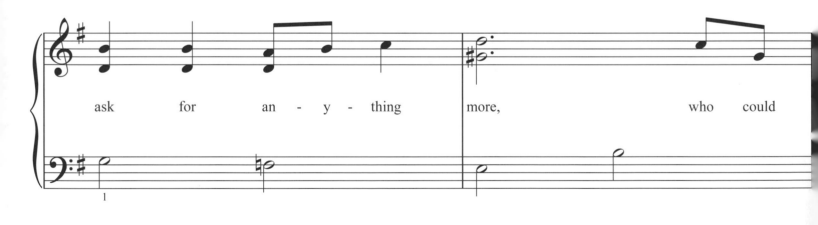

ask for an - y - thing more, who could

ask for an - y - thing more? more?

WHEN SUNNY GETS BLUE

Lyrics by JACK SEGAL
Music by MARVIN FISHER

like the wind that stirs the trees. Wind that sets the leaves to sway - in'

like some vi - o - lins are play - in' weird and haunt-ing mel - o - dies.

Peo - ple used to love to hear her laugh, see her smile; that's how she got her

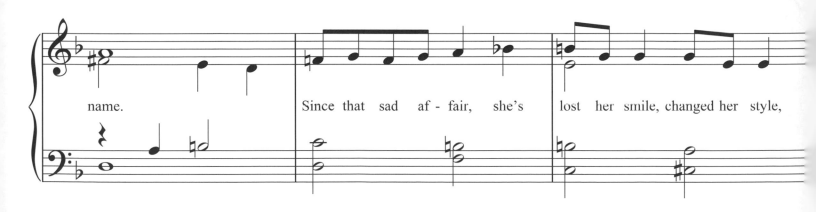

name. Since that sad af - fair, she's lost her smile, changed her style,

some - how she's not the same. But mem - 'ries will fade, and

prct - ty dreams will rise up where her oth - er dream fell through.

Hur - ry new love, hur - ry here, to kiss a - way each lone - ly tear, and hold her near, when Sun - ny gets

blue. Hold her near, when Sun - ny gets blue.

rit.

STARDUST

Words by MITCHELL PARISH
Music by HOAGY CARMICHAEL

Moderately slow

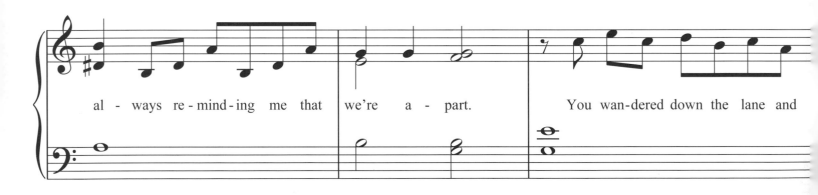

Love is now the star-dust of yes-ter-day, the mu-sic of the years gone

by. _____ Some-times I won-der why I spend the lone-ly

night dream-ing of a song. The mel-o-dy

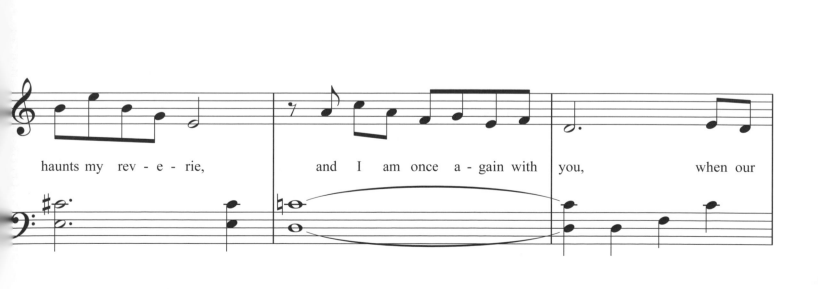

haunts my rev-e-rie, and I am once a-gain with you, when our

love was new   and each kiss an in - spi - ra - tion.

But   that was long a - go; now   my con - sol - a - tion is

in the star - dust of a song.   Be - side a gar - den

wall when stars are bright,   you are in my arms. The

night - in - gale   tells his fair - y tale   of par - a - dise, where ros - es

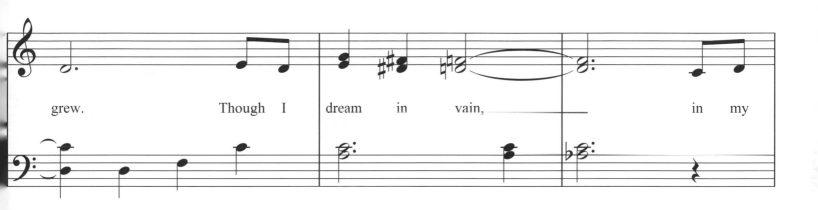

grew.   Though I   dream in vain, _____   in my

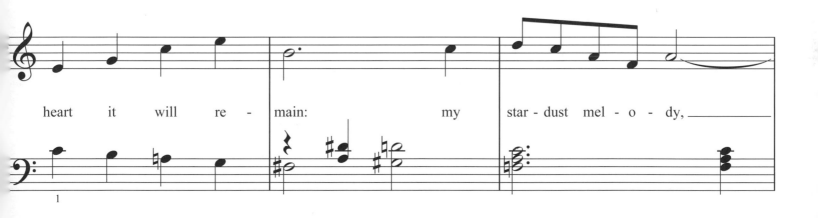

heart it will re - main: my   star - dust mel - o - dy, _____

_____ the mem - o - ry of love's re - frain.

rall.

MOONLIGHT IN VERMONT

Words by JOHN BLACKBURN
Music by KARL SUESSDORF

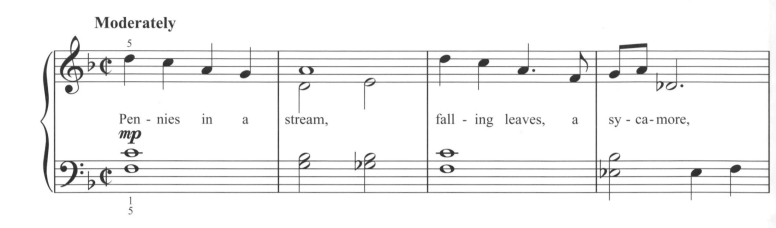

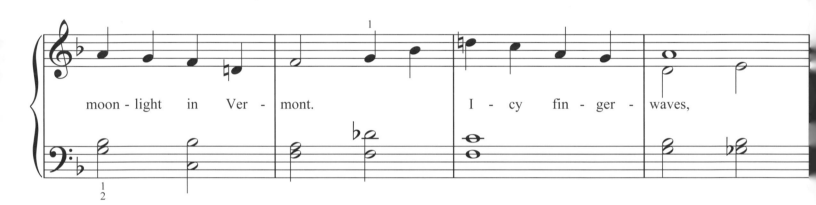

TAKE FIVE

By PAUL DESMOND

To Coda ⊕

D.S. al Coda

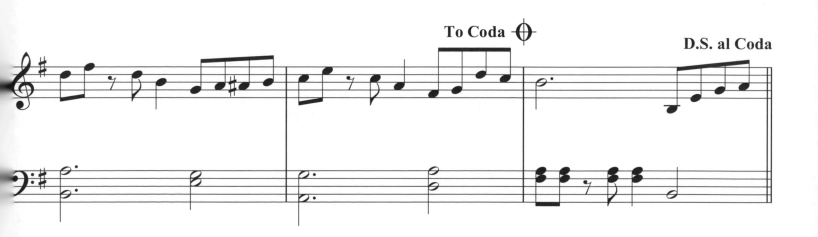

CODA

SPAIN

By CHICK COREA

Freely, rubato

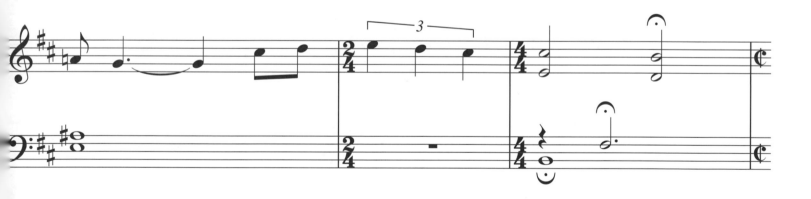

Bright Latin Tempo

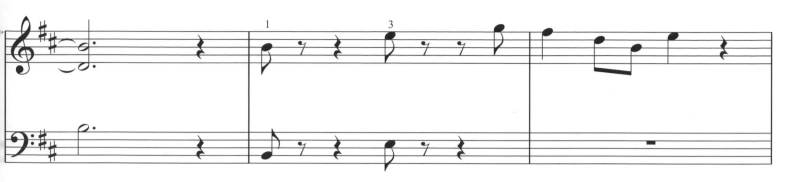

To Coda ⊕

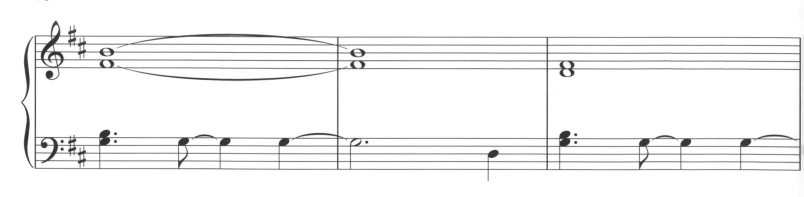

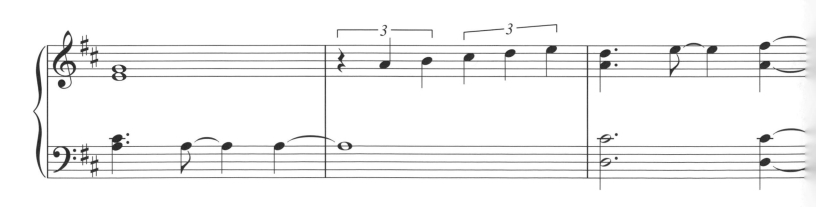

D.S. al Coda

CODA

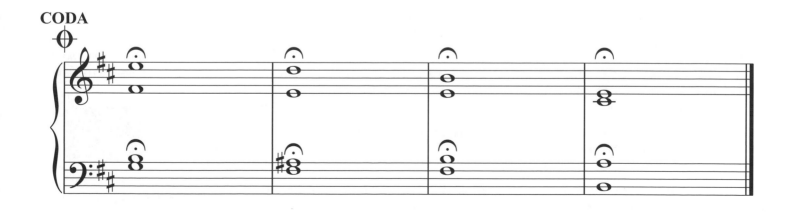

FIRST 50

You've been taking lessons, you've got a few chords under your belt, and you're ready to buy a songbook. Now what?
Hal Leonard has the answers in its **First 50** series.

These books contain easy to intermediate arrangements with lyrics for must-know songs.
Each arrangement is simple and streamlined, yet still captures the essence of the tune.

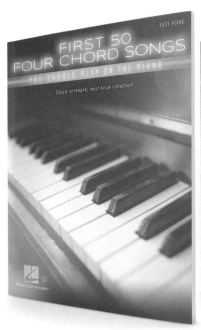 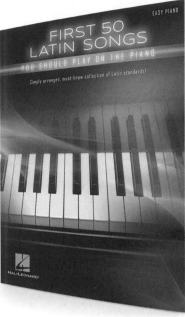  

First 50 Songs by the Beatles You Should Play on the Piano
00172236 Easy Piano......................$19.99

First 50 Broadway Songs You Should Play on the Piano
00150167 Easy Piano........................$14.99

First 50 Christmas Carols You Should Play on the Piano
00147216 Easy Piano........................$14.99

First 50 Christmas Songs You Should Play on the Piano
00172041 Easy Piano........................$14.99

First 50 Classic Rock Songs You Should Play on Piano
00195619 Easy Piano........................$16.99

First 50 Classical Pieces You Should Play on the Piano
00131436 Easy Piano Solo................$14.99

First 50 Country Songs You Should Play on the Piano
00150166 Easy Piano........................$14.99

First 50 Early Rock Songs You Should Play on the Piano
00160570 Easy Piano........................$14.99

First 50 Folk Songs You Should Play on the Piano
00235867 Easy Piano........................$14.99

First 50 4-Chord Songs You Should Play on the Piano
00249562 Easy Piano........................$16.99

First 50 Gospel Songs You Should Play On Piano
00282526 Easy Piano........................$14.99

First 50 Jazz Standards You Should Play on Piano
00196269 Easy Piano........................$14.99

First 50 Kids' Songs You Should Play on Piano
00196071 Easy Piano........................$14.99

First 50 Latin Songs You Should Play on the Piano
00248747 Easy Piano........................$16.99

First 50 Movie Songs You Should Play on the Piano
00150165 Easy Piano........................$14.99

First 50 Pop Ballads You Should Play on the Piano
00248987 Easy Piano........................$16.99

First 50 Pop Hits You Should Play on the Piano
00234374 Easy Piano........................$16.9

First 50 Popular Songs You Should Play on the Piano
00131140 Easy Piano........................$16.9

First 50 R&B Songs You Should Play on Piano
00196028 Easy Piano........................$14.9

First 50 3-Chord Songs You Should Play on Piano
00249666 Easy Piano........................$16.9

Prices, content and availability subject to change without notice.
www.halleonard.com

0